Hamsters and Guinea Pigs for Kids

Amazing Animal Books for Young Readers
Compiled By: Molly Davidson
Mendon Cottage Books

JD-Biz Publishing

Read More Amazing Animal Books

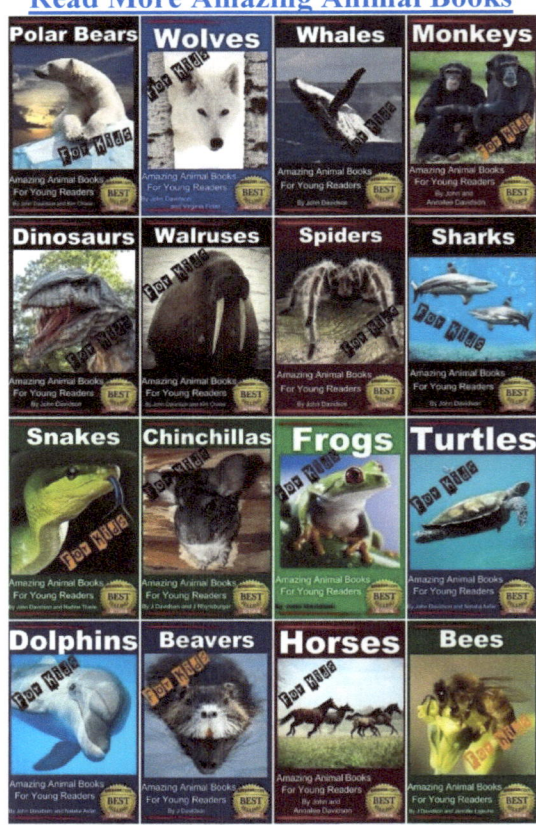

Purchase at Amazon.com

Download Free Books!
http://MendonCottageBooks.com

Table of Contents

Introduction

Hamsters and guinea pigs both make great pets.

They both are usually covered in hair and have four legs.

So what is the difference between a hamster and a guinea pig? Let's read and find out.

Guinea Pigs

Guinea pigs are some of the cutest pets around, with a history going back thousands of years. Nowadays, guinea pigs are popular pets among many people.

The guinea pig is not only adorable, but a cornerstone of the Andean civilizations; there is so much more to guinea pigs than their current position as a very popular pet for company, showing, and breeding. In places outside of modern society, they still hold a place in the rituals and healing of many peoples.

As a pet more delicate than rabbits or cat, or especially dogs, the guinea pig survives as it is due to thousands of years of breeding and protection by humans.

The guinea pig is an animal that has captured the imagination of many people, from Beatrix Potter and C.S. Lewis to the ancient peoples of the Andean area. Hopefully, it will capture your imagination as well!

What is a guinea pig?

A guinea pig is not a pig, despite its name. It is a rodent, related most closely to capybaras and maras. It also doesn't come from Guinea, which is an area in Africa. Instead, it comes from the area in South America around the Andes mountains, in places such as Colombia, Panama, and other such countries.

A guinea pig on the grass

Guinea pigs are also called cavies, and are related to a number of wild animals called cavies. However, guinea pigs barely exist in the wild; it is said that there are a number of escaped guinea pigs that are known as wild cavies, but it's unknown when they escaped and how many of them there are.

Most guinea pigs that have lived as pets would not know how to survive in the wild. This is pretty normal for most pets, but for the guinea pigs especially.

A guinea pig looks a bit like a little furry log; their shape is kind of like a pill. Unlike some of their relatives, guinea pigs can't sit back on their hind legs and use their front legs to eat; instead, the guinea pig holds down food with their front paws, and bites into it with their mouth.

Guinea pigs have long front teeth, called incisors, that are very strong and can bite through some tough things. These are used to cut the food, while their back teeth grind things up. There is a space between the incisors and the back teeth, called a diastema.

Another thing about guinea pigs is that they have a variety of sounds they make. One example is the noise often called the 'wheek.' It's a little whistle sort of noise, and guinea pigs often make it when they're excited. If they see their beloved owner or are getting fed, they may make this noise. Another reason might be to find another guinea pig.

Guinea pigs also purr, or make a sound similar to a purr. This is a noise that means the guinea pig is delighted; like with cats, they may make this noise when being petted. They may also make it when being fed. Guinea pigs love to be fed.

A sign that a guinea pig is angry or afraid is a sound known as a 'rumble.' It's similar to purring, except that it's shorter and a lower sound. Sometimes, males will use this to enforce their dominance (control) over the other guinea pigs.

A chattering sound is a bad sign; this means the guinea pig is giving warning. If a guinea pig is making this noise with its teeth, it's usually best to back off.

However, a sign there is a real problem is when the guinea pig shrieks or squeals. This means they are reacting to pain or great fear. If they are making this noise, it's important to investigate or immediately remove the problem.

Guinea pigs are very focused on food. When it comes to food, they can learn complex ways to get to it. They are not as intelligent as their cousin, the rat, but they can remember pathways to food for a very long time.

They are also very social animals; it is a cruelty to keep a single guinea pig. If a person does keep more than one guinea pig, the most likely groups to work are any number of females, or females and one male. It's not a good idea to keep a number of males together.

Guinea pigs tend to groom each other, and get along well with each other.

Guinea pigs have also shown an ability to get along with other animals. This can mean they can get along with dogs, cats, birds, almost anything, but it often doesn't happen with predator animals.

People are divided on whether or not it is a good idea to house rabbits and guinea pigs together, but often, if they are kept together from a young age, guinea pigs and rabbits can share a cage or hutch.

What kinds of guinea pigs are there?

Many, many types. While there aren't exactly separate species of guinea pig, there are many kinds of breeds. This includes breeds with special hair, different colors, and other things.

A long-haired guinea pig

Often, they are grouped by their coats, or their fur.

First off, there's the smooth coated group. This is the most common kind as pets for your average family, as they don't require extra care. They have smooth, soft fur, and it's generally short.

This includes short haired guinea pigs, which are the most simple kind of guinea and most match the wild cavies. They have smooth, soft coats, and they come in many colors.

Ridgebacks, on the other hand, are quite similar except for a ridge of fur standing up on their backs. It often looks like a mountain ridge, uneven in the way it stands up.

Another type of smooth coated guinea pig is the satin. This kind of guinea pig has glossy, smooth fur that is incredibly soft to the touch. However, satin coats are often linked with disorders, so it's hard to breed a healthy satin, in some ways.

Second type of guinea pig: long coated guinea pigs. This type of guinea pig has long fur, and there are several more types of it than there are smooth coated guinea pigs.

An example is the silkie. This is a type of guinea pig that has soft, long fur. For it to be considered a well bred silkie, it must not have a part, or have any rosettes (swirls of fur that look vaguely like roses), and its fur must not point towards its face. It looks like a big puff of hair.

A texel is similar to a silkie, but instead, its coat is curly. There's debate between English and American breeders as to the kind of curl it should take, but some say it is the rex version of the silkie (a rex cat has curly fur).

Another long coated guinea pig is the lunkarya. This is a new kind that is popular in the Nordic countries (such as Sweden, Denmark, and Norway). It has a very dense, curly coat, and comes in several types, depending on whether or not it has a forelock (which is hair that comes over the face), a coronet (which is fur that frames the face) or its coat is tear drop shaped from above.

A second new breed is the Sheba. It has rosettes all over its fur, and is often called a 'bad hair day' guinea pig. It's only really recognized as a breed in Australia.

The third type of coats for guinea pigs is the rough-haired. This includes the rex, which has short rough hair, the Abyssinian, which has similar hair with rosettes added in, and the teddy, which resembles a stuffed toy.

The last kind is the hairless. There are only two types: the skinny pig, which has hair on its face and nowhere else, and the Baldwin, which has hair when it's born, but loses it as it gets older.

There are a number of types of colors and patterns for guinea pigs. Sometimes guinea pigs are a solid color, like black, chocolate, red, or white. This is called being self-colored.

There's also a pattern called 'ticked', which means the hairs are both red and black.

Then there are also several patterns. A couple include the Dalmatian, which is similar to a Dalmatian dog, and tortoiseshell, which has patches of red and black.

There's a large variety to guinea pigs, but all are mostly the same build-wise.

Where did guinea pigs come from?

Guinea pigs were domesticated (made tame) by humans thousands of years ago, with some saying they have been domesticated since 5000 BC. This happened in the Andean area, long before Europeans came, among the native peoples.

A Southern mountain cavy, a relative of the guinea pig

This means that guinea pigs were domesticated some time after the alpaca and the llama. However, their main purposes are different: where the llama and the alpaca are used for their fibers (their coats) and other things, the two main purposes of the guinea pig is as food, and as medicine.

In fact, guinea pigs have long been popular in this area as food; there's an attempt, in current times, to try to spread the guinea pig as a source of food, but most people in first world countries find it disgusting.

The guinea pig was used as folk medicine too, and still is in some isolated areas. A guinea pig is typically rubbed against the sick person to help heal them. It's said to aid the cure.

Guinea pigs are relatives of the modern wild cavies, including, for example, the Southern mountain cavy, as pictured above. Because they have been separate for so long, however, a guinea pig is distinctly different. A small example is that most wild cavies are brown, whereas a guinea pig comes in many colors and coat types.

Guinea pigs live on in Andean society; guinea pigs are used in many sayings and proverbs, and there are many pieces of art with guinea pigs in them. Guinea pigs are entrenched in the Andean cultures.

In modern day places like Colombia and Panama, you can still find plenty of roasted guinea pigs to eat.

The history of guinea pigs and humans

Since guinea pigs were domesticated a long time ago, it was a simple matter for the guinea pig to become popular in Europe, and then all over the world, from its humble beginnings in the Andean area.

A girl with her guinea pig

European explorers came upon the cultures in the Andean area. They changed a lot of things, and sent a lot of things home; one of these things was the guinea pig. Since guinea pigs survive well in enclosed spaces, they were able to handle being transported on ships.

After that, they became the rage in Europe. Like their cousin the rat would be, they were prized pets for the upper class, and breeding them for coat appearance began. There had already been some breeding done by the Andeans, but breeding for show began with the Europeans.

Guinea pigs spread across Europe, and their place as a pet was cemented. Not once did these people think of eating their exotic pets.

There is some debate over where the name 'guinea pig' comes from. Guinea is an old name for a place in Africa, which they obviously don't come from; guinea was also a name for a type of coin. So, some say their origin was confused, others that they could be bought for a guinea.

As for pig, it's likely their ability to live in pig pen type conditions led to the name, or perhaps that they heard of the locals herding them like pigs. No one knows for sure.

However, sometime around the 19th century, guinea pigs became popular animals for testing medical ideas on. Using them as test subjects had started long before then, but it picked up in the 1800s. Soon enough, they were as popular as rats and mice for the same purpose.

Guinea pigs were (and still are) used for many purposes. For example, the Soviet Union and China have sent guinea pigs into space, and they were used to discover many things in gemology.

The term 'guinea pig' often means that the thing or person called that are being tested on. For example, if you were trying out cutting people's hair for the first time and you practiced on your sister, your sister would be your 'guinea pig.'

Nowadays, most test animals are rats or mice; the guinea pig is used rarely, especially since about the middle of the 1900's.

Sometimes, people are allergic to guinea pigs. They may be allergic to their urine and other bodily fluids, or they may be allergic to their dander.

Breeding guinea pigs

Breeding guinea pigs has been a hobby (and sometimes a profession) since guinea pigs were first brought over to Europe. Guinea pigs only gained their many different breeds from people with time on their hands and the passion to want to create new breeds.

A hairless guinea pig

Nowadays, guinea pig breeding is a hobby that can be a lot of fun, but also a lot of work.

The key with guinea pig breeding is to make sure the parents have traits that will translate well; you can never know for sure how mating two guinea pigs will turn out, but you get a better chance if you choose healthy parents. It also helps to match breeds, if you want to produce pups that are one breed.

Guinea pigs can breed all throughout the year, though they're most likely to breed in the spring. Guinea pigs are pregnant for a little more than two months, typically.

When a female guinea pig is pregnant, she usually takes on a shape like a squash. This is because the pups can be very large, and often the guinea pig may have a large litter. The larger the litter, the more likely it is that there will be stillborn pups.

Unlike most rodent babies, guinea pig pups are born with a coat, some eyesight, and the ability to move around, among other things. They are not completely helpless like mice, rat, and squirrel babies.

Another thing that pups can do immediately is eat solid food; however, they still rely on their mother for nursing until they are weaned.

Like elephants, a female guinea pig will usually be willing to adopt abandoned pups. They are also willing to help with the nursing if a mother has a lot of pups. So, unlike with large litters in other animals, it's very rare for a young guinea pig to end up not getting enough milk.

Female guinea pigs can carry a litter before she's reached a full adult age; however, the danger for females (who have a metabolic disorder) if they don't have babies before six to ten months of age is that they may have calcification (hardening) of their pubic symphysis, which is what stretches to allow babies out. If this hardens, it will be harder for her to give birth.

There are not as many complications with pregnancy for guinea pigs as there are for some other animals. A danger is always toxemia, but this can be caught: a mother will have anorexia (where she won't eat), lack of energy, and fruity smelling breath.

The male guinea pig doesn't have as many potential problems as a female guinea pig does. They don't contribute to parenting, though any other female in the cage might. When the females work together to raise young, this is called "all parenting."

Show guinea pigs

Guinea pigs, like most domestic animals, can be highly involved in shows. Guinea pigs bred to look just so, to fulfill their breed's highest rules for appearance. They are also groomed and such to look just right.

A long-haired guinea pig

In a show, the guinea pig will have had its coat brushed and made to look nice for the judges. A guinea pig is judged on things like coat quality and its closeness to breed standards.

The standards for guinea pigs are decided by clubs. There are clubs in many countries, but the main one in America is the American Cavy Breeders Association. This one is a branch off of the American Rabbit Breeders Association, rather than being its own association. It also is used by Canadian breeders.

In the United Kingdom, the main organization is the British Cavy Council. And there are similar organizations in Australia and New Zealand.

Different clubs have different standards for breeds. What is a breed in one place is just a mutt in another; where the Texel is expected to have tight curls in one, they're expected to have brushed out curls in another. There is no universal standard for any breed.

For shows, guinea pigs with short hair are often brushed a couple times a week, whereas a long haired guinea pig may need daily grooming. All of this prepares them for shows.

At shows, unlike at dog shows, they are not judged on anything they do, but entirely on appearance. Guinea pigs are not generally trained to do tricks.

Guinea pig showing is a lot of fun. It's a reward for a lot of hard work.

Guinea pigs as food

Guinea pigs are known as cuy in Andean cultures. Once upon a time, they were only eaten for special occasions, but more recently they've become normal to eat as a staple.

They are much better as food for poor families than pigs or cattle because they are small, they reproduce fast, and they can live in much smaller spaces. The meat is often the only meat in a family's diet, and meat is important to be healthy (at least, protein is, though there aren't a lot of sources in their society).

There are several ways to cook guinea pigs. They can be fried, broiled, or roasted, and they can go in casseroles or be part of a barbecue. Some use them in soups.

Guinea pigs are such a big part of Ecuadorian cuisine (the food people from Ecuador eat) that there's a painting of the last supper (the last supper of Jesus Christ before he died) that shows Jesus and his disciples eating guinea pigs.

They are also eaten in some parts of Africa. No one knows for sure when the guinea pigs were brought over, but they've proved to be a boon for poor African households for the same reasons they are great for poor South American households. Guinea pigs aren't counted among livestock surveys, so no one knows how many there are in Africa, but they've spread quite a bit.

However, in Western culture (such as America, Canada, Great Britain, France, etc.), it is not considered a good thing to eat a guinea pig. It would be like someone cooking and eating their dog to most people in Western culture.

A little more on guinea pigs

From the Disney movie *G-Force*, which features superhero guinea pigs, to the sweet guinea pigs in Beatrix Potter's work, guinea pigs have caught the imagination of the world for a long time.

Their humble origins as little cavies served to make them the fashionable pet of the Europeans and others, and then into the cute, loveable pet of today.

Guinea pigs love their owners, and learn to recognize them, a lot like a dog or cat; they are the perfect pet for small spaces. The guinea pigs' popularity, which it has enjoyed for a long time, will only continue to grow into the future.

If you've ever considered having a guinea pig, they're not a bad pet to start out with. They live longer than hamsters, and are considerably more cuddly. However, they aren't the same kind of commitment as a dog or cat. If a friend has a guinea pig, it's probably worth seeing if you like them by visiting and playing with your friend's pet.

However, always remember that your parents have the final say, and listen to them.

Facts about Hamsters

Hamsters are fuzzy little creatures that are easy to care for. There are many fun facts about hamsters. There are over 25 different hamsters in the world but only five can be kept as pets. The biggest hamster is 34cm or 12 inches long and the smallest hamster is about 51/2 cm or 2 inches long. Hamsters are easy to take care of. The oldest hamsters live up to four years old. They can live for two, three or four years.

The heart of a hamster beats between 300 and 500 times in a minute. They have teeth that keep growing just like the teeth of rabbits. That is why they keep munching and biting stuff. It is important to give them dog biscuits to prevent them from biting the bars of their cage. They also need their toenails to be clipped using a nail cutter. If the hamster bites, try to put sandpaper on the base of their running wheels so that it can file the nails when the hamster runs.

Hamsters have a good memory. They can remember other hamsters that are related to them. They also respond to names. When you call your hamster by name, it will come to you. There is a hamster type called the Syrian hamster that comes in forty colors. If you love different colors, try keeping the Syrian hamster for a pet. Remember to keep a male hamster in its own cage. Keep two male hamsters into two different cages. Male hamsters fight and bite each other when they are kept together. These are some amazing facts about hamsters.

How Hamsters Communicate

Hamsters are those cute puffy little animals that you can hold into your hands. Like us, humans, each hamster has its own distinctive personality which makes it unique in the hamster's world. What all the hamsters have in common is the way they communicate with each other. You can actually observe if you are paying attention if your hamster is angry, happy or he is simply in a mood to spend some time alone.

Hamster communication is quite amazing - they emit a certain smell when they rub up against objects, they squeak and have a specific body language. When your hamster smells an object, it means he marks his territory. When he squeaks, it means he communicates with other hamsters. If there is no other animal around, this means your little and cute pet is afraid of something or has a state of discomfort. Lastly, when he stretches his body, this means your pet is relaxed or, in case it is a female, she is interested in mating.

Hamsters as Pets

You go to a pet shop, and all of a sudden you discover there's a small furry animal called a Hamster. You are about to ask your parents to buy you one, when you realize it is a good idea to find out more about having hamsters as pets.

At first glance, you might think it is a mouse, but when you look again, you see its rounded body, and immediately notice their beautiful colors, such as brown, beige, ivory, and some of them are spotted as well. You would love to have one of them at home. Having hamsters as pets is not a bad idea, but keep in mind that hamsters are not toys. They are recommended when children are eight or older. These little animals like to sleep during the day, that's why it is important to manage them (under adult supervision) carefully so they won't bite you.

Hamster Care

Hamsters, aren't they among the cutest things you have ever seen? They are wonderful and cuddly pets that young boys and girls like you love to own. Because of their small size and nature, they are fairly easy to take care of.

Let's go through some of the things you need to do to ensure that your hamster remains a happy and healthy little fellow.

1. Spacious habitat

The home of your furry little friend should always be one that is very spacious and large. This is so that the little guy has room to move around and doesn't feel cramped up in its cage.

2. Filling the cage with essentials

Now that we have a home in place, it then has to be filled with all the things that the hamster will need. They include: bedding (which can be bought at the pet store), a water bottle, a food dish, some toys and of course the hamster running wheel.

3. Proper feeding

As with most hamsters, you will need to keep them on a diet that consists mostly of vegetables, fruits, seeds and nuts. However, it is recommended that you mainly feed them the readily available food mixes for hamsters. On occasion, you can also feed them some apple, bananas, spinach and sweet potatoes.

4. Health

The best way to ensure that your pet remains healthy, is to always clean up after him/her and also make sure that he/she has enough toys to keep them busy and active.

That's it. If you do those things and do them well, you will always have a happy and healthy pet.

Hamster Health

It is very important to keep your hamster as healthy as possible if you want it to be happy and feel at home living with you. I will now go over some simple tips to keep your hamster healthy.

Housing - One thing your hamster will love is having a lot of room in its cage to explore, you also want to have a wheel for your hamster to exercise on as this will keep it fit and healthy.

Cage - Make sure you keep the cage away from windows or any bright lights.

Food and Water - Be sure to make sure the water you give the hamster is fresh and at room temperature, make sure it is not too hot or cold. Also try not to feed any leftover vegetables to your hamster as some have been sprayed with chemicals that can damage the hamster's health.

I hope these tips have helped you make your hamster healthier.

Hamster Food

Feed your little hamster well to keep him healthy

A hamster is small and fragile so it's very important to feed him properly. He mostly eats grains and seeds like: sunflower seeds, corn, barley, maize, pumpkin seeds or peanuts. It's better to feed him the mixes that are found in pet shops because those are rich in vitamins and give him a good diet.

There are some treats that he can eat sometimes. Green vegetables are his favorites. Feed him cauliflower, lettuce, broccoli, spinach or cucumbers and you will make his day. He also likes dried fruits, biscuits, toast, dried cheese or sugarless cereals.

Never share your own food with the hamster. He needs special food. No chocolate, candies, chips or pickles. He is not allowed to eat foods that contain water because he will have stomach issues. Also, he can't eat almonds, grape seeds, fruit stones, apple seeds or spices.

The hamster has to eat hamster food mixes that are specially made for his needs.

Hamster Balls

Hamsters have become very popular in recent years because it does not require special care and get along well with children. There are dozens of species of hamsters, in different colors, with long or short fur but only 5 of them are kept as pets. If you have a hamster then you need to buy him a hamster ball.

Hamster balls are a pretty good way to ensure your hamster movement required, but you must know how to use it to prevent some problems. Choose a hamster ball that fit comfortably. The diameter of 17 cm are good for dwarf hamsters, but Syrian hamsters need bigger balls with a diameter of 28 cm. Hamster not have to arch the back to run the ball. It must necessarily be equipped with air ventilation holes .Always supervise when the hamster ball. Make sure you are headed towards some stairs, and no other animals are nearby the hunt hamster ball. In addition, it is fun for you to watch the hamster that runs the ball.

Hamster Cages

Hamsters are small and cheerful little creatures. For a comfortable life, they need a cozy and spacious hamster cage completing the necessary items and accessories. If your pet is completely satisfied with the cage, one can watch him. Soon his lifestyle and habits will become one of your favorite hobbies.

Hamsters love to move around and play. Therefore, hamster cage should be large. Two-story hamster cells with different ladders will be interesting and attractive, not only for animals but also for the owner - you can not only watch, but to play along with these funny creatures.

In the hamster cage, it is advisable to put a small shelter. Pet will rest here and make a pantry for food storage.

In the hamster cage should be feeder and water. Choose for your pet metal or wooden toys, as they are more durable.

Finish "hamster home" is not necessary, place all the necessary items in the cage; the hamster will do the rest himself.

Types of Hamsters

There are different kinds of hamster available in the world. They range from larger to smaller animals. They are in the same class of animals with the dogs but are small.

Each breed of hamster has different characteristics. For example, we have the Syrian large hamster type. This type is the most common type of hamster. It Lives for about 3 years. This is the ideal pet for any child. We also have the dwarf Russian hamster. This is the smallest of all hamsters. This is the most social with one another. They make the best pet. Because of their size it is hard for small children to handle them. The other type is dwarf Russian hamsters. They are social with one another. They come from China. They are lively but hard to handle. It lives for about 2 years. All The hamsters have different colors. Some are purple to white in color.

Dwarf Hamsters

The dwarf Russian Hamster is smaller than the Syrian or Golden hamsters kept in regular mode. Adult males reach only up to 8 cm. Hamster in captivity lives best in pairs or in small groups. The life of a dwarf hamster is 2-3 years, but can reach 5 years. You can give them almost anything, but do not give them fruits and vegetables such as cabbage, onions, garlic, potatoes, grapes and every kind of citrus. Do not give them chocolate because chocolate may affect the respiratory system of the hamster. Dwarf hamsters are able to sneak through boxes for normal hamsters, so you need to buy a cage with smaller spaces between the bars.

There are three species of dwarf hamsters:

Russian dwarf hamster: Originally from Central Asia, China, Mongolia and Russia, Robo dwarf hamster: originally from Central Asia , China, Mongolia and Russia is the smallest of hamsters, reaching a length of 5 cm and the White Dwarf Hamster Syrian: originally from eastern Siberia and Kazakhstan

Russian Dwarf Hamster

Russian dwarf hamster is usually active at night and it is ideal for children of 10 years and above. These hamsters have high energy levels and they are social within the family. They have a lifespan of three years. They are approximately 3 to 4 inches long with males being slightly larger than their female counterpart. They also have a bullet shape. These hamsters have thick hair which encloses their feet and have a short-haired coat. They are available in varieties of colors and can be housed in groups or same-sex pairs when all of them are raised together.

With consistent interaction, Russian dwarf hamsters are easy to tame and once they are tamed, they become curious, confident and friendly to human beings. These hamsters like moving around and so it is vital to provide them a large room for their movement even though they are small. The front teeth of these hamsters never stop growing; therefore, they should be given healthy meals to chew.

Syrian Hamsters

Syrian hamsters are available in different colors which make them amazing pets for adults and children. They are the most popular hamster species often kept as pet. These hamsters originate from the Middle East particularly Syria and Russia. These hamsters are currently classified as endangered species. Syrian hamsters are approximately 13 cm in length; however, some are a little bit larger. The females are usually larger than their male counterpart. They have tulip shaped ears, large eyes and a short tail. Syrian hamster is sometimes referred to as 'the Golden Hamster'.

Original wild color of these hamsters is golden brown but the body's upper two thirds is black. The fur in the belly is white with a gray undercoat. In the wild, females only tolerate the males during mating but attack the male at any other time. These hamsters are solitary animals and therefore, they should be housed alone. These hamsters are bred in four coat types which include Satin, Long haired, Rex and Short haired.

Teddy Bear Hamsters

Teddy bear hamsters are small and very cute pets

Hamsters are lovable and popular pets. A very nice type of hamsters is the Angora hamsters, which are also known as 'teddy bear hamsters'. They can have lots of different nice colors. Also, they have a very soft fur, which is quite long compared to other types of hamsters.

Take care of them well and they will be happy and healthy. Don't feed them something else but seeds and occasionally fruits or greens. The water must be fresh every day. Their home should be a big cage with a ball, pieces of wood for him to chew and different toys.

These little puffy pets love attention. Play with them very much. Just make sure that they don't escape. They are very fast and it will take a lot of time to catch them. You should only be a bit careful when they is sleeping. You shouldn't bother them because they might get scared and bite you.

Teddy bear hamsters are adorable and it's really enjoyable to have them as pets.

Winter White Hamsters

The winter white hamster comes from Asia and parts of Europe. It is smaller than other hamsters and is usually called a dwarf.

The winter white hamster has fury feet and the rest of its body is covered with shorter fur. Its color is usually either dark or light grey. This winter white hamster also has a darker stripe on its back. This stripe runs from the back of its head to its tail. This hamster is called winter white because in the winter, the color of its fur changes to white.

Winter white hamsters are usually kept in Europe and North America as pets. These hamsters are easy and good to keep as pets because of their gentleness. They are usually very active and run around a lot. Winter white hamsters give birth to many pups at once, which means that they will need a lot of space to live in.

Conclusion

I hope you have learned many facts about hamsters and guinea pigs. Now you should know the difference, and this may even help you decide which you would like to have as a pet.

Read More Amazing Animal Books

Purchase at Amazon.com

Top Ten Dog Breeds For Kids

Amazing Animal Books For Young Readers
Kisha Bennett & John Davidson

German Shepherds

Dog Books for Kids
K. Bennett

Bulldogs

Dog Books for Kids
K. Bennett

Dachshund

Dog Books for Kids
K. Bennett

Poodles

Labrador Retrievers

Dog Books for Kids
K. Bennett

Rottweilers

Dog Books for Kids
K. Bennett

Boxers

Dog Books for Kids
K. Bennett

Dog Books for Kids
K. Bennett

Golden Retrievers

Dog Books for Kids
K. Bennett

Puppies
Dog Books For Kids

Amazing Animal Books
By John Davidson

Beagles

Dog Books for Kids
K. Bennett

Yorkshire Terriers

Dog Books for Kids
K. Bennett

Dogs
Top Ten Dog Breeds For Kids

Amazing Animal Books For Young Readers
Zahra Jazeel & John Davidson

Cats For Kids

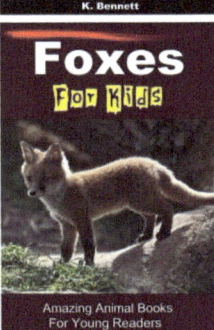

Amazing Animal Books For Young Readers
K. Bennett & John Davidson

Foxes For Kids

Amazing Animal Books For Young Readers
Zahra Jazeel & John Davidson

Wolves For Kids

Amazing Animal Books For Young Readers
By John Davidson and Virginia Fidler

Our books are available at

1. Amazon.com
2. Barnes and Noble
3. Itunes
4. Kobo
5. Smashwords
6. Google Play Books

Download Free Books!
http://MendonCottageBooks.com

Publisher

JD-Biz Corp

P O Box 374

Mendon, Utah 84325

http://www.jd-biz.com/

www.ingramcontent.com/pod-product-compliance
Lightning Source LLC
Chambersburg PA
CBHW040311010626
45792CB00022B/172